TECHNOLOGY IN
THE ANCIENT WORLD

ANCIENT EGYPT

BY CHARLIE SAMUELS

W
FRANKLIN WATTS
LONDON·SYDNEY

First published in Great Britain in 2015 by
The Watts Publishing Group

Copyright © 2015 Brown Bear Books Ltd

All rights reserved.

For Brown Bear Books Ltd:
Editorial Director: Lindsey Lowe
Managing Editor: Tim Cooke
Children's Publisher: Anne O'Daly
Art Director: Jeni Child
Designer: Lynne Lennon
Picture Manager: Sophie Mortimer

Dewey no. 932

ISBN: 978 1 4451 4261 6

Printed in China

Franklin Watts
An imprint of
Hachette Children's Group
Part of the Watts Publishing Group
Carmelite House
50 Victoria Embankment
London EC4Y 0DZ

An Hachette UK company
www.hachette.co.uk

www.franklinwatts.co.uk

CONTENTS

INTRODUCTION

The civilisation of ancient Egypt lasted for over 3,000 years – far longer than the time that separates our modern world from the year 0. During that time, the peoples of the Nile Valley made huge technological advances. They used the knowledge of earlier peoples, such as the Mesopotamians. But they also made their own discoveries, such as how to build smooth-sided pyramids or how to preserve the bodies of the dead. They preserved important people as mummies.

The pyramids at Giza are among the largest and most famous examples of ancient building technology anywhere in the world.

This painting shows rowers on an Egyptian boat. The Nile was Egypt's major highway, and goods and people travelled by boat.

Such technology often changed in a series of gradual improvements, rather than in great steps or dramatic inventions.

KINGDOMS AND DYNASTIES

Egypt was formed around 3100 BCE. The king of the Nile Valley conquered the kingdoms of the Nile Delta and unified the country. Egyptian history is usually broken into periods. The Old Kingdom, Middle Kingdom and New Kingdom were times of relative peace. The country was ruled by pharaohs, or kings, from different dynasties, or families. These times were separated by less stable Intermediate Periods, when dynasties competed for power. This book will introduce you to some of the most important examples of the technology behind Egypt's remarkably long history.

TECHNOLOGICAL BACKGROUND

The ancient Egyptians pioneered new technologies but they also used the technologies of the earlier inhabitants of Mesopotamia (present-day Iraq) and Persia (Iran). These peoples included the Sumerians, Babylonians and Assyrians. The ancient Egyptians grew plants and kept animals. Most importantly for a desert kingdom, they made full use of the

Early Egyptian pyramids like this one at Saqqara were based on the stepped temples of Mesopotamia.

The Sumerians introduced cuneiform, a form of writing that used wedge shapes pressed into soft clay.

waters of the River Nile. Around 3500 BCE. the potter's wheel was invented in Mesopotamia. Later, the wheel for vehicles developed from this. The Egyptians had little use for vehicles because they had few roads, but the potter's wheel was vital to their civilisation. Cuneiform writing existed in Mesopotamia by 2400 BCE. The Egyptians copied the idea of writing and created their own form, called hieroglyphs.

TEMPLE BUILDING

The ziggurat (stepped) temples of Mesopotamia inspired the pyramids of ancient Egypt. The Egyptians' early attempts to build pyramids ended in failure. The architects did not calculate the size of the base or the angles of the pyramid sides correctly. A number of early pyramids collapsed.

THE NILE

Egypt lies in a desert. Its lifeblood is the River Nile, which flows through the country to a large delta on the Mediterranean Sea. Apart from a few oases west of the Nile, Egypt is very hot and dry. It is not an obvious place for humans to live. However, the Egyptians knew how to use the waters of the Nile.

The Nile gave the ancient Egyptians water, irrigation for farming and a reliable highway for transportation.

Riverside settlement

Egyptian towns were built along the riverbank, where transport was easier.

Every year the River Nile flooded between July and October. The flood left a black layer of fertile mud. The rich silt of the Nile meant farmers could grow crops such as barley and wheat. Every year, the flood was different. Too much water and homes were washed away; too little, and the crops failed.

MEASURING THE FLOOD

To monitor the flood, the Egyptians built nilometers. These were vertical stone columns with regular markings to measure the height of the river. Knowing the height of the flood let the Egyptians plan their annual planting.

TECHNICAL SPECS

- Desert covers more than 90 per cent of Egypt.
- The rising waters of the Blue Nile and White Nile caused the annual flooding where they met just north of Khartoum, Sudan.
- Floodwaters spread silt over the land for about 10 kilometres (6 miles) on each side of the river.
- The building of the Aswan Dam in the 1960s finally stopped the annual flooding of the Nile.
- One type of nilometer consisted of a flight of stone steps that led down to the water, such as the one on Elephantine Island in Aswan.

AGRICULTURE

This tomb painting shows a farmer milking a cow. The Egyptians drank milk and also used it to make butter and cheese.

The Egyptians called the desert the 'Red Land'. Even surrounded by desert, they were able to grow a surplus of grain on their 'Black Land', which made them wealthy. Farming depended on the Nile and its yearly flood, or inundation. The Egyptians also used irrigation to make the land suitable for agriculture.

Apart from rulers and priests, almost everyone worked on the land. The main crops were emmer wheat and barley. The Egyptians made them into beer and bread, which were the staples of their diet. Other crops included leeks, onions, beans, figs and vines. Farmers also grew flax, which was made into linen.

SIMPLE TOOLS

Farming tools were simple. The soil left by the flood was easy to turn, and ploughs were pulled by hand or by oxen. At harvest time, farmers cut grains by hand, using sickles made from wood inset with teeth made of flint (stone).

TECHNICAL SPECS

- Crops were only planted once a year, after the flood.
- Egyptian farmers divided the year into three seasons:

  Akhet (inundation): From June to September, the Nile flooded and no farming was done. Farmers made or mended their tools, or worked on building projects.

  Peret (growing season): From October to February, the fertile soil left by the flood was ploughed and crops were planted.

  Shemu (harvest): From March to May, crops were harvested.
- Women and children worked in the fields and helped harvest the crops each year.

An agricultural scene

Grain is harvested with sickles

Olives are harvested for oil

A scribe records the harvest

Oxen pull ploughs

IRRIGATION

Egyptian agriculture depended on irrigation, the manipulation of water to grow crops. In turn, that depended on people understanding the flood of the Nile. Water was stored in large, low-lying areas of land called basins. To get water to the furthest fields from the river, the Egyptians built canals and used a device called the *shaduf*.

Canals carried water to fields, allowing Egyptian farmers to use land quite far from the Nile itself.

The Egyptians constructed huge, flat basins with earth banks next to the Nile to grow their crops. They diverted water from the river when it was at the peak of its flood. This meant they could trap the water in the basins. The water stayed in the fields for 40 to 60 days before it was drained off at the right moment in the crop-growing cycle.

LIFTING DEVICE

Water was also stored in canals between the fields. To lift water from the canals, farmers used the shaduf. The shaduf was a bucket on a pole with a counterweight. It is still used for irrigation today.

TECHNICAL SPECS

- Nilometers gave farmers early warning of the height of the Nile flood. That meant they could plan how much land to irrigate and prepare the basins.
- The Egyptians adopted the shaduf from the Fertile Crescent of Mesopotamia.
- The flow of water into the basins was controlled by a series of gates (simple sluices).
- Farmers made sure there was enough water to prevent salts building up in the fields.
- A steady water flow prevented silting in the canals.

HOW TO...

The shaduf was based on the lever. A fulcrum was placed about a fifth of the way along a long pole. The counterweight balanced the weight of the water. A gentle swinging motion turned the pole and emptied the water from the bucket.

Fulcrum to support the pole

Counterweight

Bucket

WRITING

Hieroglyphs were based on pictures. They were used for official purposes, such as inscriptions on monuments.

Writing appeared in Egypt around 3000 BCE. It made it easier to organise society and pass on information. The first Egyptian writing was hieroglyphs, which were based on pictures. Later the hieratic and demotic scripts were developed for daily use. They were quicker to write than hieroglyphs.

Reading and writing was the job of the scribes. All Egyptians of high rank, including pharaohs, trained as scribes. Training took about five years and started as early as nine. Scribes learned about 700 different hieroglyphic symbols by copying texts. The symbols were pictures that could represent either whole words or individual sounds. Hieroglyphs were carved or painted on monuments, temples, tombs and religious scrolls.

EASIER ALPHABETS

For business and legal documents, letters and stories, scribes used the hieratic script. The demotic script was for daily use. It grew out of the hieratic script around 650 BCE. It remained in use for more than one thousand years.

TECHNICAL SPECS

- Only about 1 per cent of Egyptians could read and write.
- Hieroglyphs were carved in stone or painted inside tombs, which is why they have been preserved.
- Hieratic script ran from right to left. It was written using a reed brush on papyrus.
- Demotic script continued to develop between c.650 BCE and the fifth century CE.
- In 1799, Jean-Francois Champollion deciphered hieroglyphs on the Rosetta Stone. The stone had the same text in three scripts: Greek, demotic and hieroglyphs.

This statue shows a scribe at work. Scribes were highly valued in Egyptian society and many held high rank.

MATHS AND MEASURING

Building a pyramid

Blocks moved up
earth ramp to
top of pyramid

Scribe

Architect

Stone blocks
moved on
wooden rollers

Architects used precise calculations to work out the size of a pyramid's base and the angle of its sides.

The Egyptians relied on mathematics. They needed to count how many livestock they had. They wanted their buildings to stay up and not collapse, so they had to calculate the angle at which to build their pyramids. That relied on accurate calculations and problem solving. Around 3000 BCE, the Egyptians first used numbers bigger than 10.

Cubit

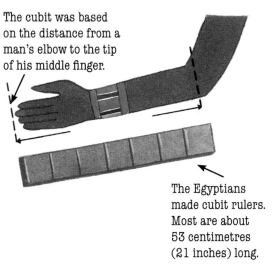

The cubit was based on the distance from a man's elbow to the tip of his middle finger.

The Egyptians made cubit rulers. Most are about 53 centimetres (21 inches) long.

- Papyri (documents) from 1990 to 1800 BCE are the first evidence of the Egyptians' skill at maths.
- A papyrus written in 1650 BCE includes calculations for building a pyramid and shows how to work out fractions.
- The number 1 was depicted by a single stroke; 2 was represented by two strokes and so on.
- The numbers 10, 100, 1000, 10,000 and 1,000,000 had their own hieroglyphs.
- The hieroglyph for 100 was a coiled rope; 1,000 was a lotus flower; 10,000 a finger; 100,000 a frog. A million was represented by a god with his hands raised.

The Egyptians used the decimal system of counting we still use today. It was probably based on the 10 fingers. There were symbols for decimal units up to one million. They added and multiplied by two. To multiply bigger numbers, they repeatedly doubled or halved, then added the results together.

UNITS OF MEASUREMENT

To measure length the Egyptians used the cubit. It was based on the distance from a man's elbow to the end of his middle finger. To measure shorter distances, the cubit was broken into smaller measurements: the smallest was just a finger wide. They used stretched-out lengths of flax as a ruler.

Water clock

The Egyptians measured time by letting water drip out of a bowl.

PAPYRUS

One of the greatest technological advances of the Egyptians was the invention of paper. They used the papyrus (a type of reed) that grew all along the banks of the Nile. Papyrus was versatile and strong. Its fibre was used to make baskets, sandals, ropes, boats, mattresses and even perfume.

Papyrus grew widely along the banks of the Nile. It was an all-purpose material for the Egyptians.

HOW TO...

Turning papyrus into paper was a skilled job. The plant fibres had to be kept damp while they were worked, then dried thoroughly before the paper could be used.

Papyrus is harvested

Two layers of strips are laid at right angles

The stem is cut lengthways into narrow strips

The layers of strips are hammered until they fuse into a sheet, which is then polished

The most valuable product of papyrus was paper (the word comes from 'papyrus'). The thick green stems of the papyrus were harvested, and the outer fibres were peeled off. The paper maker sliced the core of the stalk into long, thin strips. The strips were soaked in water to remove the sugar they contained.

FINISHING THE PAPER

The strips were laid side by side, with another layer placed on top crossways. They were then covered with linen, pounded with weights and left to dry. Once the strips were dried, the linen was removed. The paper was finished by polishing it with a shell or some ivory.

TECHNICAL SPECS

- The younger the papyrus plant, the finer the quality of paper it produced.
- Pens for writing were made from reeds. The end was squashed to make a pointed nib, which was dipped in ink.
- Black ink was often used for official documents. It was made from soot from the bottom of cooking pans mixed with gelatin, gum and beeswax.
- Different coloured inks were made from minerals that were ground into powder and then mixed with water when used. Ochre was used to make red ink.

BUILDING

An Egyptian town

Most Egyptians lived close together in small houses built of mud bricks. They had flat roofs that were used for storage and as work spaces. People cooked food in dome-shaped ovens in open yards.

Dome-shaped ovens for cooking

Pillars supporting upper storey

Pottery storage jars

The Egyptians used stone to build temples, pyramids and monuments. They got the stone from the Egyptian desert, which had deposits of limestone, sandstone and granite. Cutting and transporting stone was difficult, so it was only used for important buildings. Ordinary homes were made from mud bricks.

Among the most important buildings along the Nile were the huge temples the Egyptians built to honour their gods.

RAISING AN OBELISK

Temples contained many monuments, such as obelisks. Obelisks are four-sided pillars that taper to a point. Some were very tall. To stand them up, the builders probably built a brick funnel around the base and filled it with sand. They dragged the obelisk up a ramp so its bottom end rested on the sand. As the builders removed the sand, the obelisk tipped into a standing position. Once it was upright, the ramps and funnel were removed.

Egyptians were experts at quarrying, moving and using large blocks of stone for their religious buildings.

TECHNICAL SPECS

- To cut limestone slabs, workers hammered wooden wedges into the stone. Then they soaked wedges with water so the wedges expanded, splitting the rock.
- A brick maker could make more than 1,000 mud bricks a day. It took five days to make enough bricks for a worker's home.
- Wood was valuable. It was used for doors and window shutters in houses. The most common wood came from the palm tree.
- The Egyptians had toilets but no drains. They emptied their sewage onto fields as fertiliser.
- They transported stone on barges along the River Nile.

PYRAMIDS

Some 4,500 years after it was built, the Great Pyramid of Giza (Khufu's pyramid) still stands. The Egyptians wanted to build tombs for their rulers that reached to the heavens. Their pyramids were remarkable building feats. They remained the tallest structures anywhere on Earth for centuries.

The ancient Egyptians buried dead rulers beneath pyramids from about 2630 to 1630 BCE. The largest pyramids were at Giza.

Pyramids at Giza

Tombs of high officials

Cross-section of the Great Pyramid showing internal passageways

Temples linked to a pyramid by a causeway

Great Sphinx

How the Egyptians built the pyramids remains a mystery. They were aligned on a perfect north–south axis long before people had invented the magnetic compass. The four sides of the base were always equal in length. Workers built ramps next to the pyramid and dragged stone blocks up on sledges. Blocks at the top were probably put in place with levers.

BUILDING BLOCKS

Workers quarried the stone blocks from the desert. They shaped them and labelled their position in the pyramid. The blocks were taken by boat to the building site along the Nile.

TECHNICAL SPECS

- As many as 100,000 workers built the Great Pyramid at Giza.
- The stone blocks weighed up to 14 tonnes (15 tons). They were marked in the quarry to show their position in the pyramid.
- The builders used copper pickaxes and chisels, granite hammers and other stone tools.
- Pyramids were finished with a layer of limestone on the four sides and gold on the apex (pointed top).
- Each side of the Great Pyramid is about 230 metres (755 ft) long. There is only a 20-centimetre (8-in) difference between the longest and the shortest sides.

PRESERVING THE DEAD

The Egyptians preserved the dead in a procedure called mummification. They were not the only ancient people to do this – the ancient Peruvians also did it, for example. However, the Egyptians perfected the method of preserving a body. They believed the dead person needed his or her body to live on in the afterlife.

Mummies were wrapped in linen bandages before being placed inside a coffin. Animals were also sometimes mummified.

HOW TO...

Once the body was dried out, it was wrapped in linen. Magic charms called amulets were wrapped in the linen to protect the body. The mummy was placed in a coffin and then inside a sarcophagus, which was a richly decorated stone or wooden case.

Priest wearing a mask of Osiris, god of the dead

Magic amulets wrapped in the linen

Coffin enclosed inside wooden and stone sarcophagi

Box with jars holding organs

TECHNICAL SPECS

- The earliest Egyptian mummies were buried in hot sand, which absorbed the bodily fluids that cause a body to decompose.
- From around 4500–4100 BCE, bodies were wrapped in linen soaked in resins.
- The body's organs were preserved in canopic jars.
- The heart was not removed. It had to be weighed by Osiris, the god of the underworld, as the dead person went to the next life.
- The brain and the contents of the skull were removed through the nose using a long, thin hook.

A COMPLEX PROCEDURE

Mummification took thousands of years to perfect. Around 2600 BCE, the Egyptians learned that removing the internal organs helped to stop the body rotting. The organs were preserved separately. By 1500 BCE, the hollow body and the organs were dried for 40 days in natron (a type of salt). The skin was sealed with resin, wax and oil to keep out moisture. The body was stuffed with sawdust and leaves to keep its shape. Then it was carefully wrapped in strips of linen and prepared for burial.

SHIPBUILDING

The Nile was Egypt's highway. There were no roads, and the wheel was not used there until around 1600 BCE. The river flowed from south to north. It was used to transport everything from the huge stones needed to build temples and pyramids to livestock, grain and passengers.

Large single sail

Thick rope kept hull rigid

Oars for steering

Cargo piled on open deck

Ships were used to carry cargo up and down the Nile, but larger vessels also made ocean going voyages.

Cargo boat

New Kingdom boat

Sail is wider than it is tall

Front lookout post

Rear lookout post

Deckhouse

Wooden hull

Egypt lacked trees, so the first boats were not made from wood but were rafts made from reeds. These rafts developed into ships with hulls, and later had masts for sails and deckhouses. Wooden ships were built from imported acacia or cedar. There were no nails or pegs, so planks were tied together with papyrus ropes.

SAILING THE OCEANS

Ships had flat hulls to avoid the shifting sandbanks of the Nile. The larger wooden vessels, or feluccas, were capable of sailing on the ocean. They were used to trade with other peoples, such as the Phoenicians, and sailed to the tip of Africa.

TECHNICAL SPECS

- Ships used sails to travel upstream on the Nile, and oars and the current to travel back downstream.
- To make a ship, carpenters lashed together thousands of wooden planks using ropes of papyrus.
- Boats were sometimes buried near pyramids for the dead to use as transport in the afterlife.
- The Egyptians built the world's first lighthouse at Alexandria. It was 100 metres (330 ft) tall and was visible from 50 kilometres (30 miles) away.
- The heaviest cargo was carried on long, narrow barges towed by other vessels.

ASTRONOMY

The astronomical ceiling in the temple of Hathor at Dendera shows the gods passing across the night sky.

The Egyptians were expert observers of the night sky. Many of their important gods and goddesses were associated with the stars and planets. Priests used detailed maps of the stars during ceremonies. From observing the Sun, the Egyptians developed a 365-day calendar.

Astronomy developed separately in Upper and Lower Egypt before the two kingdoms were united around 3100 BCE. In Lower Egypt, astronomers built a circular wall to create a false horizon. On the wall they marked the position of the Sun as it rose each day. From their observations, they worked out a solar calendar based on a year of 365.25 days.

LUNAR CALENDAR

In Upper Egypt, astronomers used a lunar calendar. It was based on the Moon and the star Sirius. They noted that Sirius rose in a direct line with the rising Sun once every 365 days.

TECHNICAL SPECS

- The Egyptians understood the difference between stars and planets.
- They identified five planets: Mars, Saturn, Jupiter, Venus and Mercury.
- The first recorded date in Egyptian history – 4241 BCE –was when the Egyptians devised the 365-day calendar.
- The sun god Ra became a major god from 2500 BCE onwards. He inspired the Egyptians' view of the pharaoh and his powers.
- Nut was originally the goddess of the night sky; later she became goddess of the sky in general.

Astronomers at work. By carefully observing the night sky, the Egyptians made a highly accurate calendar.

CALENDARS AND CLOCKS

As early as 4241 BCE the Egyptians devised a calendar. This was a lunar calendar, based on the cycles of the Moon. However, the calendar could not predict the most important event in the year: the annual flooding of the River Nile. Instead, priests introduced a new calendar based on the movement of the Sun. It was more reliable.

Sundial

The Egyptians used various devices to tell the time. They measured the length or position of shadows cast by the Sun.

Crosspiece casts shadow

Plumbline checks position

Holes mark position of shadow

This clepsydra (water clock) had a tiny hole in the bottom that allowed water to trickle out.

Priest-astronomers noticed that the Nile flooded a few days after the star Sirius appeared shortly before sunrise. They based a new calendar on the Sun, with months based on the cycles of the Moon.

DIVIDING THE DAY

The Egyptians divided the day and night into 12 hours each, but the length of an hour varied with the time of year. They invented clocks to measure the passage of time. From 1500 BCE they used sundials to measure shadows cast by the Sun. Water clocks were the first timepieces that did not rely on the Sun or stars. Water trickled out of a stone jar marked with 12 'hour' sections.

TECHNICAL SPECS

- The ancient Egyptian calendar was made of weeks of 10 days. Three weeks equalled a month (30 days) and four months made a season (120 days).
- Three seasons created a year of 360 days; the remaining five days of the 365-day calendar were feast days.
- To measure the past, the Egyptians used divisions of time based on the reign of their kings.
- The Egyptians were the first people to divide the day into 24 'hours', but they were not of equal length.
- The clepsydra, or water clock, allowed Egyptians to measure the passage of time in their homes.

METALS AND MINING

The famous mask of Tutankhamun, the boy king who reigned from 1333 to 1323 BCE, was made from gold with lapis lazuli inlay. Gold and silver vessels, masks, weapons and ornaments have been found in Egyptian tombs. Gold, silver and copper could be found as nuggets in rocks, sand and in riverbeds.

The mask of Tutankhamun was made to cover the face of the mummified dead king in his tomb.

- The earliest-known travel map shows the route to a gold mine in the Eastern Desert.
- The Egyptians used copper from 4000 BCE. Iron use dates from around 900 BCE. While gold was common, iron was rare.
- Copper ore was mined from deserts between the Nile and the Red Sea.
- The Egyptians added carbon to iron to make steel.
- They hardened steel by plunging the hot metal into cold water, then reheated it to toughen it.

The Egyptians could cast complex shapes, such as this three-legged container for burning perfume, or incense.

The Egyptians obtained most metals by mining. Underground mining started in Nubia in around 1300 BCE. Mining was dirty and dangerous, and prisoners were often forced to do this work.

METAL HISTORY

The Egyptians made their weapons and tools from copper. They invented bellows around 1500 BCE, which created higher temperatures in furnaces. Metal-workers melted tin with copper to produce bronze to make weapons, tools and pots and pans. They were also able to smelt iron.

MEDICINE

Egyptian doctors wrote remedies on papyrus scrolls that survive today. They had cures for tumours and eye disorders, and carried out surgical procedures. Any sickness was treated with a prayer to a god or goddess and by priests saying magic spells. Although doctors existed, medicine was a new profession.

An Egyptian makes an offering to a god. Such offerings were a common response to illness.

A doctor treats an eye infection in this illustration from a series of images of medical treatments.

TECHNICAL SPECS

- The Egyptians wore amulets as charms to ward off illness.
- Bronze surgical knives have been found, but were probably used in mummification, not in surgery.
- The Egyptians understood that the pulse and heart were linked. They believed that thinking took place in the heart.
- The Egyptians knew the position of the vital organs from their treatment of dead bodies.
- Imhotep, an adviser to King Djoser (2630–2611 BCE), was one of the first physicians and became the god of medicine.
- Dentistry began in around 2650 BCE. Hard grain and sand in bread ground down teeth, so toothache and gum disease were common problems for ancient Egyptians.

The ancient Egyptians had an advanced understanding of the human body. Doctors knew that the body should be kept clean to prevent infection, and they also knew that eating well was linked to good health.

MEDICAL PRACTICES

The earliest-known surgery took place in 2750 BCE, although no internal surgery was performed. Doctors reset broken bones and dislocated joints. The Egyptians believed the human body was like the Nile: it had channels running through it that carried air, water and blood. If a person was sick, it was a sign that the channel was blocked and needed unblocking.

WEAVING AND DYEING

Flax grows next to a lake. The Egyptians wound flax fibres into threads and wove them to make linen.

Egyptian farmers grew flax alongside their grain crops. Flax was used to make linen for clothing. Converting the flax plant into linen was a long process. The threads were then woven on looms. The earliest-known picture of a loom dates to around 3000 BCE. Linen was dyed using an array of minerals to make different colours.

Flax was collected in bundles and soaked in water to break down the tough outer parts of the plant. It was beaten with wooden mallets to separate the fibres, which were spun on sticks (spindles). The spindle had a weighted circular whorl on one end. The spinner set the spindles spinning on the ground. This pulled the fibre from the flax and twisted the thread around the spindle. It was now ready for weaving.

DYEING

Dyes were made from various minerals. Red came from iron oxide or ochre, pale blue from copper carbonate and green from malachite.

TECHNICAL SPECS

- The weaving of cloth dates back approximately 7,000 years.
- The earliest looms were horizontal. Pegs were hammered into the ground to make a rectangular frame fitted with crossbars to hold the threads. The weaver crouched on the ground to work the loom.
- The vertical upright loom was introduced in around 1500 BCE.
- People of high rank and the rich wore the finest linen.
- The very finest linen was almost transparent; it was worn only by the pharaohs.
- Wool was also widely used to make fabric and clothes.

HOW TO...

The vertical loom replaced the horizontal loom for weaving in the New Kingdom. A wooden frame supported the threads, which were tied with weights to keep them taut. The cross-thread was pushed back and forth between the vertical threads, then pushed up into place.

Wooden upright frame

Stone weights pulling on threads kept tension

GLASS-MAKING

This scarab (lucky charm) mixes coloured glass and semi-precious stones. It was buried with Tutankhamun.

The ancient Egyptians called glass *aat wedhet*, which means the 'stone that flows'. By 4000 BCE, they had learned how to mix natron with sand and the mineral malachite to make a green-coloured glass. They used glass to make decorative containers and as beads to replace semi-precious stones. Glass was highly valued, however – it was not used for everyday objects.

The Egyptians originally made glass without realising it. They ground a mixture of alkali and silica into a powder, which they mixed with water to make a paint. They brushed the paint onto a soft stone, called steatite, and then heated it until it turned into a shiny glaze that was turquoise in colour. It was only around 1450 BCE that glass-makers from Syria showed the Egyptians that this glaze was glass and could be used in many ways.

TRUE GLASS

The Syrians showed the Egyptians how to shape glass. First they made a clay mould, which was attached to a metal rod. Layers of glass were built up around the mould. It was rolled on a stone slab to make the surface smooth. Once it had cooled, the clay core was removed and an empty glass vessel remained.

TECHNICAL SPECS

- When sand and natron were heated and became liquid, dirt sank to the bottom and froth to the top. When the liquid had cooled and hardened, the dirt and froth were broken off. What was left became the glass.
- Different minerals were added to make colour: tin oxide for white, cobalt for dark blue, antimony for yellow and copper for green.
- To make round beads, glass-makers coated glass paste onto strong thread and formed it into a bead shape. The thread burnt away in the kiln, leaving each bead with a hole for threading.
- Egyptian glass was heated to 800°C (1,470°F). Today, pure silica is heated to 1,700°C (3,090°F).

This glass jar held kohl, which was used as eye make-up. The rich blue colour of the glass comes from cobalt.

POTTERY

The Egyptians needed containers of all kinds to store food and drink and to eat and drink from. For everyday use, they used vessels made from clay. Early clay pots were made by hand. For special objects, a material called faience became widely used both for vessels and for more decorative tiles.

When the Egyptians began making pottery plates and bowls some 5,000 years ago, they moulded clay around shaped pieces of wood and left it to dry. They did not develop the potter's wheel until a few centuries later. The earliest form of the potter's wheel was relatively slow. It was turned by hand.

This glazed pottery bowl is decorated with images of fish and lotus flowers.

Early Egyptian pots like this lidded jar were made from coils of clay that were smoothed together.

In around 3000 BCE the Egyptians invented the fast wheel. It worked by using the energy – momentum – stored in a rotating stone wheel. The wheel was turned and charged with energy by kicking it or pushing it with a stick.

THROWING A POT

The fast wheel enabled a new type of pottery: a 'thrown' pot. A lump of clay was put on the rotating wheel and then worked into the shape of a vessel with thin walls. The pot was fired in a kiln at a high temperature to make it hard.

TECHNICAL SPECS

- The potter's wheel was a horizontal spinning disc. It was probably invented in Mesopotamia.
- The kiln was invented by the ancient Chinese. It was first used in Egypt around 5,000 years ago. Pots could be fired at much higher temperatures than if they were simply left to dry in the Sun.
- Faience was a type of ceramic made from crushed quartz or sand with a small amount of lime or ash. Water was added to make a paste, which was then shaped. The Egyptians usually added a blue-green colour glaze to faience.

WEAPONS AND WARFARE

Chariot charge

The chariot and the composite bow were both introduced to Egypt by the Hyksos people. An archer rode on the plaform of the chariot with the charioteer. The lack of space meant he needed a shorter bow than ordinary soldiers used. By using a composite bow, he could generate the same amount of power from a shorter weapon.

Charioteer protects archer with shield

Protective covering for horses

The most important weapons of ancient Egypt were the bow and arrow and the chariot. In around 1800 BCE, the Hyksos people of Asia invaded Egypt; they eventually ruled the Nile Delta for centuries. They brought horses, the chariot and a new kind of bow, all of which were adopted by the Egyptians.

The Egyptian bow could shoot up to 190 metres (625 feet). The more powerful composite bow of the Hyksos people could shoot a further 80 metres (260 feet). It was made of layers of wood, horn and sinew. Arrows were made of reed with flint heads; copper heads were used from around 2000 BCE.

THE CHARIOT

The chariot probably originated in Syria. The Egyptians made the vehicle lighter and quicker. The charioteer and an archer stood on a wooden platform at the back.

The army of Pharaoh Ramses II in camp: a chariot is repaired as foot soldiers drill nearby.

TECHNICAL SPECS

- During the 18th Dynasty (1550–1295 BCE) the Egyptian Army was divided between infantry and chariotry.
- Chariots were made from wood and leather and pulled by two horses. One soldier drove the chariot, while an archer fired arrows from his bow.
- Chariot wheel rims were covered in leather.
- Egyptian armour was made from leather and bronze.
- As technology improved, daggers were made from bronze and copper.
- The composite bow was given more tension by being bent backwards as it was strung.

Army camp

Body of chariot made from light basketwork

Bronze axe   Leather armour   Hide shield

TIMELINE

ALL DATES BCE

c.5000 The Predynastic Period begins in Egypt.

4241 Egyptian astronomers begin the first calendar.

c.3700 Egyptians learn to extract copper from ore by smelting it in furnaces. The copper is used to make tools.

c.3500 Farmers use ploughs pulled by cattle to prepare fields so they can plant barley and wheat.

c.3100 King Menes of Upper Egypt conquers Lower Egypt, unifying the country and beginning the Archaic Period.

c.3000 Papyrus made from reeds is used as a surface for writing.

c.2700 Egypt's bronze age begins as smiths learn how to make bronze.

c.2649 The Old Kingdom begins.

c.2630 The first Egyptian step pyramid is built for King Djoser.

c.2600 Bodies have their organs removed and are dried in natron before they are turned into mummies.

c.2590 The Great Pyramid at Giza is built for the Pharaoh Khufu.

c.2500 The Egyptians develop a system of sluices and canals to control the floodwaters of the Nile.

c.2400 An Egyptian artist paints an image of a potter's wheel in use.

c.2150 The First Intermediate Period begins; it is a period of relative instability.

c.2040 The Middle Kingdom begins.

c.1880 Another painting show a bellows being used to increase the temperature of a fire being used to melt metal.

c.1800 The Hyksos people of the Middle East conquer much of Egypt

c.1800 The Hyksos introduce the chariot and composite bow to Egypt.

c.1640 The Second Intermediate Period begins

c.1580 King Ahmose I drives the Hyksos out of Egypt.

c.1555 The shaduf is introduced along the Nile for raising water.

c.1552 The New Kingdom begins; it marks the strongest period of the Egyptian Empire.

c.1500 Weavers begin using vertical looms.

c.1490 Egyptians begin to make glass vessels.

c.1450 Water clocks are used to tell the time.

c.1200 Iron begins to replace bronze in tools and weapons.

c.1150 The earliest surviving map is created. It shows the location of gold-mines in the desert.

c.1069 The Third Intermediate Period begins.

c.664 The Late Period of Egyptian history begins.

c.600 Egyptian ships sail around the continent of Africa.

c.332 Alexander the Great occupies Egypt, beginning a period of Greek rule.

280 The world's first lighthouse is built at Alexandria.

197 A decree by the ruler Ptolemy V is inscribed on stone in Greek and two forms of Egyptian. This Rosetta Stone will allow hieroglyphics to be deciphered in the early 19th century.

30 Egypt is conquered by the Romans.

GLOSSARY

afterlife The place where Egyptians believed the dead went to live.

alkali A chemical compound such as lime or soda.

amulet An object used as a charm for protection against evil.

canopic jar A jar with a lid shaped like an animal head, used to hold the organs of a mummy.

chariot A horse-drawn, two-wheeled war vehicle with a platform at the back for an archer.

composite bow A bow made from fused layers of wood, bone and sinew for additional power.

faience A glazed type of ceramic.

felucca A fast-sailing ship on the Nile, with a triangular lateen sail.

Fertile Crescent A crescent-shaped region of the Middle East stretching from Egypt along the east coast of the Mediterranean to what is now Iraq.

flax A plant whose fibres are used to make a textile called linen.

fulcrum The point on which a lever is supported as it acts.

furnace An oven that generates high temperatures to melt metal.

hieroglyphs A writing system that uses pictorial symbols to stand for letters and words.

inundation The annual flooding of the Nile.

irrigation A system of artificially watering fields for farming.

kiln An oven used to harden pottery or bake bricks.

loom A frame for weaving yarns to make textiles.

mummy A dead body that has been preserved and prepared for burial.

natron A mineral salt that absorbs moisture.

ore Rocks and minerals in which metals naturally occur.

papyrus A reed whose fibres were used to make paper, also called papyrus.

pharaoh The title given to Egypt's kings and queens.

pyramid A four-sided structure with a square base that tapers to a point.

resin A sticky substance that seeps from trees or other plants.

scarab An amulet or charm in the shape of a beetle.

scribe A person who copies out documents.

silica A hard substance that occurs as the mineral quartz.

smelt To extract metals by heating their ores.

staple A food that makes up the major part of a diet.

FURTHER INFORMATION

BOOKS

Ancient Egypt (Eyewitness Project Book). Dorling Kindersley, 2009.

Bone, Emily. *Egyptian Things to Make and Do* (Usborne Activities). Usborne Publishing Ltd, 2011.

Ganeri, Anita. *Ancient Egypt* (Great Civilisations). Franklin Watts, 2014.

Malam, John. *100 Things You Should Know About Pyramids* (100 Things You Should Know About…). Miles Kelly Publishing, 2010.

Snedden, Robert. *Ancient Egypt* (Technology in Times Past). Franklin Watts, 2008.

Tyldesley, Joyce. *Egypt* (Insiders). Templar, 2007.

WEBSITES

www.ducksters.com/history/ancient_egypt.php
Ducksters pages on the people, culture and technology of ancient Egypt.

http://legacy.mos.org/quest/
Museum of Science pages about ancient Egyptian science and technology.

www.bbc.co.uk/history/ancient/egyptians/
BBC site that presents an introduction to ancient Egypt.

http://egypt.mrdonn.org
Pages about ancient Egypt on Mr Donn's social studies site.

Note to parents and teachers: In the book every effort has been made by the Publishers to ensure that websites are suitable for children, that they are of the highest educational value, and that they contain no inappropriate or offensive material. However, because of the nature of the Internet, it is impossible to guarantee that the contents of these sites will not be altered. We advise that Internet access is supervised by a responsible adult.

INDEX